T0197415

ROUND EYES

An Adopted Child's View of Love

Written by Ginger Sanders

Illustrated by Tracy Applewhite Broome

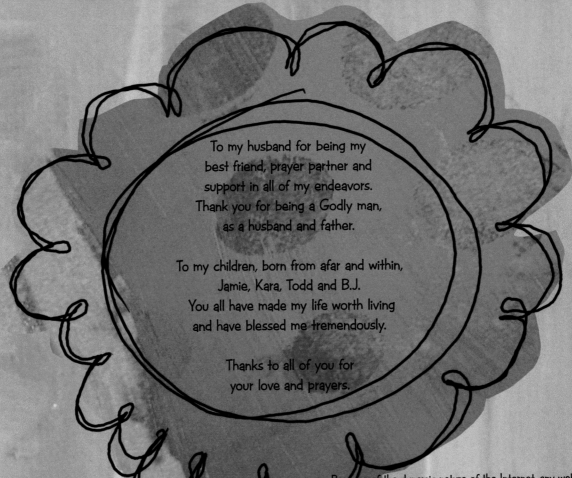

To my husband for being my
best friend, prayer partner and
support in all of my endeavors.
Thank you for being a Godly man,
as a husband and father.

To my children, born from afar and within,
Jamie, Kara, Todd and B.J.
You all have made my life worth living
and have blessed me tremendously.

Thanks to all of you for
your love and prayers.

WESTBOW
PRESS®
A DIVISION OF THOMAS NELSON
& ZONDERVAN

WestBow Press books may be ordered through booksellers or by contacting:

WestBow Press
A Division of Thomas Nelson & Zondervan
1663 Liberty Drive
Bloomington, IN 47403
www.westbowpress.com
844-714-3454

Because of the dynamic nature of the Internet, any web addresses or
links contained in this book may have changed since publication and
may no longer be valid. The views expressed in this work are solely
those of the author and do not necessarily reflect the views of the
publisher, and the publisher hereby disclaims any responsibility for them.

Any people depicted in stock imagery provided by Thinkstock are
models, and such images are being used for illustrative purposes only.
Certain stock imagery © Thinkstock.

ISBN: 978-1-5127-0386-3 (sc)
ISBN: 978-1-5127-0387-0 (e)

Library of Congress Control Number: 2015917904

Print information available on the last page.

WestBow Press rev. date: 01/29/2022

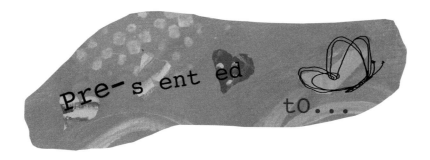

Pre-s ent ed

to....

_____

By>

_____

There once was a Mommy and Daddy that lived in a house, with a big yard and a big dog named Lady, but one thing was missing.

There were no little
boys or girls living there
in the house with the Mommy
and Daddy. The Mommy and
Daddy wanted a little boy or
girl, but did not have one.

The dog, Lady, had puppies and Lady seemed content and happy, but Mommy and Daddy did not have children.

They were lonely and wanted to share
the love and the life God had given them.

pR-aY
always
to gE the r

So one night, Mommy and Daddy prayed to God,
"God you have given us a house, you have given us a yard and
you have given us a dog and you have given us love...

but you haven't given
us a little boy or girl
to share any of those
things. Could you please
hear our prayers and
bless us with a child?"

In another land, far away, a little boy was born to a
mother who did not have a house, or a yard, or a dog. Even
though she loved her son, she could not keep him.

Jer-E mI-ah 29:11   precious ∧ba b y

She needed to find him a home. She prayed to God,
"God, can you find someone to love and raise my son?"

Through those prayers, though miles and miles away, God put the little boy on an airplane and he flew halfway around the world to his new Mommy and Daddy, house, yard, dog and her puppies.

They were all so very happy!

Then, one day the little boy drew a picture of his family...
stick Mommy and Daddy with great big round eyes
and he was the baby with little slanted eyes.

They all laughed, because even though they looked different, they all shared the house, the yard, the dogs and most of all... Love.

God's love.

I John 4:7-8
Beloved, let us love one another,
for love is from God, and whoever loves has been
born of God and knows God. Anyone who does
not love does not know God, because God is love.

Can you draw your family here?

Our Story

Round Eyes is a beautifully written story to help young readers understand the love of family—even when you do not look the same. Ginger Sanders has captured with great tenderness how it is a love and shared experiences that connect a family—in spite of differences. This sweet little book will be loved by children and their parents—for the life lesson it holds, whether or not they are adopted!

Susan Soonkeum Cox *is Vice President of Holt International Children's Services. She is recognized as a national expert on intercountry adoption and was one of the first children adopted from Korea in 1956.*

Printed in the United States
by Baker & Taylor Publisher Services